MEMORIES OF RUDOLF STEINER AND MARIE STEINER-VON SIVERS

MEMORIES OF RUDOLF STEINER AND MARIE STEINER-VON SIVERS

ANNA SAMWEBER

RUDOLF STEINER PRESS

Rudolf Steiner Press
Hillside House, The Square
Forest Row, RH18 5ES

www.rudolfsteinerpress.com

First published in English translation by Rudolf Steiner Press, 1991
Reprinted 2015

First published under the title *Erinnerungen: an Rudolf Steiner und Marie Steiner-von Sivers* by Verlag am Goetheanum, Dornach, Switzerland, 1981

Translated from German by Ursula Ruse

A CIP catalogue record for this book is available from the British Library

ISBN 978 1 85584 518 3

Cover by Morgan Creative
Typeset in Great Britain
Printed and bound by 4edge Limited, UK

Introduction

I met and got to know Anna Samweber in the 1950s. Then we did not meet again for more than ten years, when I had the opportunity to visit her for two days on 5 and 7 April 1968. At that time she was living in the Lessing-Nicolai house in Berlin.

This lady of 84 received me with a radiant warmth and was so open that she talked about her life for more than six hours on each of the days, interrupted only by a break for us to take some refreshments. When she started to talk about her memories of Rudolf Steiner I was so impressed that I started to write down, in her presence, what she related.

Originally I had not come with the intention of doing this, but found her account so important, that I felt I had to write it down there and then; also, she thought it right that the happenings she remembered should be correctly recorded. During her long life she had told her experiences to many people, in order to contribute to the creation of a true picture of Rudolf Steiner. Incidentally, the other person present at these meetings was my friend, Francis Engel.

Anna Samweber, a small, active and lively personality, related everything with great animation from her very conscious and retentive memory. As co-worker with Rudolf Steiner in Berlin for several years she had taken a very direct part in his activities. One year after our meetings she left this earthly plane.[1] *Her memories, contained in notes from Berlin, lay for years in a drawer. I spoke of them for the first time in 1977 in a lecture on the occasion of a commemoration for Marie Steiner in Zurich. The response was so positive that I have frequently been asked since to speak on these notes. With this booklet I can now meet the wishes expressed by many to put them into print. Although the stories should be taken literally, in some instances they are allegorical — my notes throughout were not a word for word transcription but purport to give an authentic sense of what was related.*

The time-lag between the present and the happenings here recorded give them today a historical character which allows us to see the personal more objectively.

Jakob Streit

The Young Governess

Anna Samweber was born on 8 June 1884, the daughter of a master baker, and grew up in Munich. She always referred to herself as the baker's daughter. After she finished school her parents sent her to a convent in northern Italy to be trained as a teacher. As a young governess she was in charge of a child in a French family. There she came into contact with the family of a German shipowner in Odessa (Crimea) where, not yet twenty, she became the teacher of the daughter of this very rich household. There was a good-sized German colony in this Black Sea port, which was served by a German school. Soon Anna Samweber was asked to teach in the school as well as continuing with her job as governess, which she did with enthusiasm and joy. Amongst her experiences in Odessa, two stand out unforgettably in her mind and are given here in her own words.

The First Experience

One warm summer day I entered the café of the German Club, in order to eat an ice-cream with my charge. Shortly afterwards a young gentleman with a poodle came in and sat at a table next to ours. The little dog was charming and we talked to him and his master who introduced himself as coming from Vienna. In the course of the conversation I mentioned that I came from Munich and that I had been away from home for some years during which I had not seen my parents. He said that he had to go to Vienna on business shortly and also to Munich and offered to take greetings from me to my parents. We arranged to give him a small present for my parents before he departed abroad. Some time later I received a letter from home full of thanks and enthusiasm about the nice gentleman and what he had had to tell them. When he came back to Odessa he came to visit me, with the lady of the house present. He showed a friendly interest in us and brought back greetings and messages from my parents. Then he suggested that we might continue our conversation in a nearby beach café, but, not being used to this sort of thing, I hesitated. However, the lady of the house took his part and persuaded me to accept his kind invitation. The summer weather was beautiful and soon we sat outside the café and chatted, while large and small boats enlivened the scene on the water. The gentleman then proposed a boat trip to round off the lovely afternoon. I felt rather strange about the whole thing and he had to be very persuasive before I followed him somewhat reluctantly. He went directly to a waiting motorboat a little way off, had a few words and, with a wink to the boatman, said I was to get in. When I noticed this I suddenly had the impulse to run away, and like a frightened animal I ran until I reached home in quite a state but also relieved.

The gentleman did not appear again, but a fortnight later the police came to the house. I was shown a photograph album with pictures of several men and asked whether I knew any of them and, indeed, the friendly Viennese was amongst them. The police told us then that they had found my address among his belongings and that this man was part of a girls' vice-ring, which had just been discovered. With some others this Viennese 'gentleman' had been caught enticing girls to a 'nice boat ride' and then taking them outside Odessa to a waiting steamer which was to transport them to the Orient, where they disappeared without trace. It had come to me like a flash of inner lightning — destiny had intervened!

The Second Experience

In 1914, before the outbreak of the war, it became known in Odessa that the Tsar's family was to pay a visit to the town. The Tsarina came from a German Royal House and German was the common language in the family. For this reason, the unexpected honour of preparing the welcome for the royal guests fell to the German school in Odessa, by entertaining them with songs and poems. There was to be a special children's reception for the Tsarina and her family, but for reasons of security the royal guests remained in the special train within the station area of Odessa.

On the day, a colleague and I turned up with the chosen group of children from the German school. I had been asked to say a few words of welcome and to direct the programme. With a small camera in my possession I asked my colleague to take a photograph of the Royal family, if it could be done unnoticed. We then arranged ourselves in rows in the carriage and admired the luxurious decor and the buffet where the sweetmeats from the confectioners of Odessa were displayed. Finally the Tsar's family arrived but without the Tsar. The Tsarina was seated in an armchair and her children stood beside her. When I started my speech in German a court official stepped in front of me and said: 'The court language is English or Russian!' So I had to adjust quickly and say my words of welcome in Russian.

The youngest daughter, Anastasia, stood directly by the buffet with the sweets and, while my children made their presentation, I noticed how Anastasia lifted the lid of a chocolate box, took a praline and put it into her mouth. She then took another one and gave it to the Tsarewich, who was standing beside her. I smiled at Anastasia, but the Tsarina noticed it, looked at them and saw the Tsarewich putting a chocolate into his mouth. She jumped up, went to him and demanded strictly: 'Spit it out, spit it out!' He obeyed immediately but Anastasia had swallowed hers already, whereupon the Tsarina gave her a slap on the hand. We were all rather shocked, but our programme continued and soon we were kindly dismissed.

However, I had the photograph which had been taken secretly and which showed clearly the family of the Tsar in the royal carriage. I always kept it with me and took good care of it, even in the war when we had to flee from Russia. Later on, the picture was to become of special interest.

Flight From Russia

My occupation as governess of the shipowner's daughter continued. Later the girl became the second wife of Trotsky. The lessons at the German school became a problem through the start of the First World War, and I had a strong desire to escape and return home. Some time previously I had acquired a little dog, a terrier, and with him, a rucksack and a little money, I started in 1915 on my way from Odessa to Munich against all better judgement. Long stretches were already war zones and without any public transport. Partly by train, then by foot and by horse-drawn wagons I arrived in Hungary with my little dog in the rucksack.

Since the money had run out I had to beg my way through, and after many weeks of hardship I came to Budapest. As I had not eaten for three days I stood by a café and the little dog helped to beg by standing on his hind legs. After a while an officer came past and looked at my shabby figure and the little dog with surprise, and when I asked for food he invited us into the café. When I told him about my plight he was very sympathetic and took me to a hotel for a few days' rest. Then he got me a ticket to Vienna, gave me clothes and a little hamper with food (There are star-hours but also star-beings — one of those he certainly was.) In stages, with long waiting in between, I travelled to Vienna. The hamper was now empty with the help of others, and eventually I arrived in Vienna. I went straight to the German Embassy, but when I told them about my adventurous escape from Odessa to Vienna they did not seem to believe me. Then I noticed the officials talking together at the back of the room and it occurred to me that they might suspect me of espionage. I therefore ran away to the Western railway station, wandered about hungry, and waited for a miracle to happen. It came in the form of a sign: *To the Station Mission, Red Cross, 2nd Floor*. When I went in, I found an officer with the Red Cross sign around his arm, eating his breakfast. My little dog sniffed and, coaxed, jumped straight onto his lap, where he got something to eat. With that, contact was made and I was able to speak about my situation. The officer thought for a while about how he might help me to get to Munich. Then he made the following suggestion: 'If I declare you to be a troublesome vagrant you will be officially deported and can travel free of charge on a German goods train returning to Munich.' I was very pleased. He issued the paper, stamped and signed it, and bade me a good journey. In this way my little dog and I travelled contentedly and happily towards Munich and my long-lost homeland.

Some years later, after the war, while I was on a visit to Dornach, I met an acquaintance near the Goetheanum. The lady was in the company of a gentleman whom she introduced as 'Dr Kolisko'. Was not a name like that signed on my vagrants' certificate from Vienna? I got the document from my handbag, where I always carried it with me, and there was the signature 'Kolisko' which I showed to the gentleman. At first, he was taken aback when it turned out that he was the officer from the Mission in Vienna — Dr Kolisko — whom I was to meet here again. Be sure we went and celebrated our reunion!

In Munich

I had been away from home for fourteen years and nobody knew I was coming. At the exit of the station my curious eyes discovered a poster which announced a lecture about education which I thought would interest me very much. When I arrived at my parents' home I wanted to enjoy their surprise fully. My parents lived in the ground-floor flat and I put the little dog in front of the door, rang the bell, slipped inside and went a few steps up the stairs. When my mother came out, very surprised to find the little dog, she fetched my father and together they puzzled over its appearance. Then I cam running down the stairs and we all enjoyed a very happy reunion.

In the afternoon my mother had an appointment to meet my sister at a certain time in the Café Luitpold in town. 'You must come, your sister will be so surprised.' So we went together into town, but my sister had not yet arrived at the café. While we were waiting I looked at the newspaper, as I had not read a Munich paper for a long time, and I also thought I would hide myself behind it when my sister came in. There I saw again the announcement of a lecture *The Education of the Child*, to be given by Michael Bauer. Education! I had to go to it. Therefore, I made mental note of the place and time.

When my sister appeared we greeted each other with great excitement and this was followed by many happy days at home together. On the evening in question I went to the lecture. There seems to be many peculiar-looking people; some also in strange dress. What I heard, though, impressed me very much; I was transported into a new world. Afterwards I tried to speak to the lecturer but he was completely surrounded by ladies so I could not get near him. Only downstairs at the exit did I succeed when he walked down in the company of a very charming person. She was Margaretha Morgenstern, wife of the poet Christian Morgenstern who, as I heard later, had died the year before. One of my questions was whether there would be other similar events to this. The lady referred me to the 'Art-studios' in Munich where Anthroposophical evenings took place and where the library, etc. was situated. Quite unwittingly I had found contact with the Anthroposophical Movement and from then on began to read books by a certain Rudolf Steiner. Since I had offered my help at once, I was asked to join in the task of bringing the card index of the Anthroposophical library up to date and so get some order amongst the books. I was also invited to help with a memorial festival which was shortly to take place.[2]

I was also told that I could help with decorating the room with flowers, and at the end of the evening stand at the door with a collecting bowl. (I was practised in begging.) As a matter of fact, I did not really know what it was all about, with these strange and yet likeable people. I only knew of Rudolf Steiner from the literature I had just started to read. Well, the evening approached; I had helped to decorate the room with red roses. A Mr Arenson began by playing the harmonium solemnly, with his little son Hans standing by his side. On the platform were several gentlemen reading a strange text.[3] The part of Benedictus was read by Rudolf Steiner, whom I did not then know. This same speaker then came onto the platform and gave the memorial address which touched me deeply. I knew then that the one who had spoken must by Dr Steiner, whose works I was currently reading. His word and message moved my innermost being. Again the harmonium sounded and I then went to the door with my collecting bowl. The crowd dispersed slowly and I put down my bowl. I saw Dr Steiner surrounded by people, in conversation, and the thought arose in me: What had to enter my life that would enable me to shake hands with this man? Normally I am anything but shy and sentimental but here I had to turn away. The tears flowed and I stood aside and waited in order to help with the clearing up. Suddenly I heard a voice behind me, and a hand, stretched out across my shoulder, took mine. It was Dr Steiner who said to me: 'Goodbye, see you in Berlin' and he laughed. I was speechless — what did I have to do with Berlin?

After about four weeks I received a letter from Cologne written by a Mrs Hummel, who often took shorthand notes of Rudolf Steiner's lectures. She wrote: 'Through a recommendation from Frau Dr Steiner I would like to ask you whether you would be prepared to work with me and Fraulein Dr Vreede in producing typescripts of Rudolf Steiner's lectures.' For this purpose she invited me to go to Cologne, and I accepted.

The book *Theosophy* served as a sign of recognition at the station in Cologne. The two ladies welcomed me very warmly and already in the tram we used the familiar 'du'. Although I was not even a member of this movement (I had read just two books by Rudolf Steiner) I was treated with the utmost courtesy.

My stay in Cologne extended to roughly three months, during which time I typed the lectures dictated to me by Frau Hummel. Then came the telegram of destiny from Berlin to Frau Hummel, asking that I go there to edit and type the winter lectures by Rudolf Steiner.

In Berlin

Soon afterwards I packed all my clothes and belongings into my Japanese basket, put a leather belt round it and travelled to the — for me — uncertain Berlin address: 17 Motzstrasse. Here was the Anthroposophical centre and also the living quarters of Rudolf Steiner and Frau Marie Steiner during the times when they stayed in Berlin. With a beating heart I climbed the stairs with my heavy baggage to the second floor. I rang the bell, the door opened, and there stood Rudolf Steiner in person. I was so taken aback that I dropped the Japanese basket which burst open and all my clothes and underclothes, together with my other belongings, were lying at the feet of the Doctor. A ball of wool got away and rolled between Dr Steiner's feet into the long corridor. Somewhat surprised , but amused, he said: 'I have never been greeted in this way.'

That was my entry into Berlin. Soon I began with the typing of lectures and other written work.

It was wartime. A crèche for children was set up and Rudolf Steiner asked me to take on the running of it, which I did without delay. There was also a hospital for wounded soldiers which a rich member of the Anthroposophical community was financing. It was of great concern to Rudolf Steiner that this was also supported by much practical help. He designed a medal which was given to the most able and willing helpers and supporters. Inscribed on it were the words: 'Hail to the helpers of healing.' The embossing showed helping hands receiving the rays of the sun in order to take them to the dark places of the earth.[4]

Christmas Plays in Berlin 1916/17

With great love and care Rudolf Steiner had resurrected the Christmas plays which had been collected by his beloved Viennese teacher Prof Karl Julius Schröer. There were performed not only at the Goetheanum but gradually in more and more places. Their presentation out of the old folklore made it possible for present-day men to experience visually and in a meaningful way the message of the birth of Christ. Rudolf Steiner was very keen on a correct interpretation and true portrayal.

In the middle of the war a group of players had come together in Berlin to perform in different towns and also in hospitals. I myself took the role of the innkeeper, wearing a national costume for the part. Once, an early morning performance in the Virchow hospital was arranged and I was in charge of the costumes and props for the actors. Very early in the morning I packed as many costumes as I could into my Japanese basket, and what I could not fit in I put on under a fur coat I was wearing so that I looked rather fat and round. It was still dark when I climbed into the bus and it was only after we had travelled a long way that I noticed with dismay we were going in the wrong direction and I got off quite upset. Because of the shortage of petrol during the war the buses ran only infrequently and taxis were only allowed within a small area. Nevertheless, I stopped a taxi and explained to the driver that I had to go to the Virchow hospital in great haste. The taxi driver looked at my round figure and noticing my agitated state told me to get in. Whatever the speed restriction must have been, he rushed me through Berlin as fast as he could. Once he asked with concern: 'Can you still manage?' Yes, I could manage. We arrived at the entrance of the hospital with only a little delay. Amongst the people waiting for me was a doctor in his white overall. When I got out somebody called: 'At last she is here.' Then the taxi driver remarked proudly to the doctor: 'Nothing has happened yet'. After all that, everybody — patients and staff — enjoyed the play.

At the beginning of February 1917 Rudolf Steiner came to Berlin for a time. In the meantime, some member in Dornach had said that in Berlin the Christmas Plays had been performed in a modified way. When I was greeted by Rudolf Steiner he said very strictly: 'Sam, call the company together, I would like to see the play.' I was rather dismayed, but it had to be. Without an audience, and with Rudolf Steiner in the front row, we performed the play that had already been abandoned two months before. I noticed how, during the performance, he swung his pince-nez excitedly to and fro and moved his leg up and down. At the end he jumped onto the stage and shouted: 'They are innkeepers and not landladies, and shepherds and not shepherdesses.' It thundered out — then dead silence. At that, I stepped forward and with the same loud voice declared: 'Herr Doctor, it is wartime, the men are on the battlefield! We now have to stand in for men!' Again, absolute silence. Then he spoke the liberating words one after the other: 'That-I-can-accept.' After that he invited us all to coffee and cake and was very warm and jolly.

Those times were wonderful — to be with him and see how he could always adjust to the situation of the moment. He always accepted every person anew and without prejudice, even if one had made mistakes.

The Call for Help

Frau Dr Steiner owned a lovely diamond watch with her initials inscribed on the lid. It was broken, and I had to take it to a well-known watchmaker who lived a long way from the Motzstrasse. It was late on a cold and foggy November evening when I made my way in the direction of Nollendorfplatz, where the building site for a subway was situated. I was walking along a long, wooden blank wall when suddenly two human shapes appeared from the dark and attacked me. I remembered that once Rudolf Steiner had told me that if ever I was in need I could call on him. So when these two attackers went for me, the one holding me from behind so that the other could rob me, I called inwardly and spontaneously: 'Doctor, help me!' At the same moment both fellows fell back like lightning and were gone.

When Rudolf Steiner came for breakfast the next morning he greeted me with the words: 'Good morning, Sam. What was the matter that you cried so loud last night?' When I told him about my experience and he had listened quietly, he said simply: 'But I did help you, didn't I?'

Local Worries

The house at 17 Motzstrasse was divided in such a way that on the first floor were situated the library of the Berlin Branch and the living quarters of Herr and Frau Walther. Herr Walther, who was a higher official of the Post Office, led the Anthroposophical work in an exemplary way. He also administered the library. On the second floor were the rooms of Dr and Frau Dr Steiner when they stayed in Berlin, as well as a eurythmy room. The third floor was occupied by the rooms of the Branch. 17 Motzstrasse was a big building complex with an inner yard and, at the time, was the home of the Anthroposophical work in Berlin. In the basement, the owner, Herr Wernicke, had established a dance school, which he ran. When he died his sons were not interested in continuing the dance school so his widow, Frau Wernicke, decided to let the rooms. The new occupier was an 'occultist' who had founded the 'Lodge of the Holy Grail'. Whoever came into the house saw, on the one side, our nameplate *Anthroposophical Society* and, just opposite, the one of the 'Grail Lodge'.

One day Rudolf Steiner arrived from Stuttgart and saw this arrangement in the entrance hall. He objected right away that it was impossible to be in the same house with this Lodge; one or the other had to leave. An arbitrator was appointed and finally the Lodge was given notice to leave, though the Anthroposophical Society had to pay the costs of the move. In this way the situation was resolved.

Frau Warnicke let the rooms anew and about two months later a ladies' club moved in. When Dr Steiner came to Berlin again I told him with mixed feelings about the new tenant, but he said: 'That is none of our business; that won't disturb us, but one has to make the eurythmists aware of it.' With that, the matter was then settled.

The New Hall

In the year 1918 the Society moved into new accommodation at 93 Potsdamerstrasse, which consisted of a lecture hall, a small stage and other rooms. At the time we moved in we had no chairs for the upper, blue hall, and a wealthy member generously donated the chairs for the hall for the benefit of the Branch in Berlin. After a lengthy absence Dr and Frau Dr Steiner came back to Berlin and arrived at the new headquarters. With great joy I showed them the upper, blue hall with the new chairs. To the astonishment of Frau Dr Steiner and myself Rudolf Steiner said 'Please, Frau Doctor, I want you to pay the amount back to the donor.' When she expressed surprise, he answered: 'You see, this Branch is the home of our work and study and must be carried by us. A donor often thinks that through a gift he gains the right to take part in decision making' — Dr Steiner made it clear that he did not want to put himself under an obligation in this case.

Marie Steiner therefore paid back the considerable sum for the chairs. Immediately after this discussion Marie Steiner had to go for rehearsal into the big hall and I stayed with Rudolf Steiner in the upper hall. He continued the conversation and said: 'You see, Sam, one cannot bequeath anything to a society. A society is something fluid. Tomorrow another person may be in charge and might do everything differently. It is only possible to bequeath something to a person or a group of people, who will then have the single benefit from it. You know it was in Weimar that the Goethe Society owned a house. In this house were the Goethe-Schiller Archives, but the Goethe Society had no say in the affairs of these Archives and its publication of the works by Goethe. I mention this as an example.'

Reproved

Since Rudolf Steiner could not be cross with people around him when they had made mistakes and in order not to disturb the relationship between teacher and pupil, he often delegated such uncomfortable duties to Marie Steiner. He called her sometimes in fun his 'cleaning woman' and once used the expression: 'She must be my broom.'

Now it happened that Dr Steiner told me off again in the presence of Frau Dr Steiner, who then said to him: 'Why are you always angry with Sam?' He answered: 'I have to be able to be cross sometimes and then I can only do it with people I know will put up with it.' I replied then: 'And I am glad when I get told off by the Doctor, because then I know that he cares for me and my work.'

The Philosophy of Freedom and the Gold

It was about the year 1917 that a new edition of Rudolf Steiner's book *The Philosophy of Freedom* was to be republished. Dr Steiner needed an old copy, but no longer had one. So he went to a second-hand bookshop opposite 17 Motzstrasse and searched for his work. After he had rummaged about without success I happened to enter the same bookshop. The ladies who worked there, and whom I knew, pointed out the heaps of books which were lying around and remarked: 'Look how he has busied himself again.' I knew that he was looking for his *Philosophy* and began myself to search. In the middle of a pile of books I found a copy.

Happily, I took my find home and said triumphantly: 'Herr Doctor, I have found something in the second-hand bookshop.'

He answered: 'But not the *Philosophy*? — I don't believe it.' 'Shall we bet on it?' 'How much?' 'Twenty marks.' Then I showed him the book and he was amazed, and he then gave me two gold coins representing ten marks each.

At that time our member Herr Hummel was a soldier stationed in barracks in General Pape Street and had no evening leave. Therefore he could not take part in the lectures by Rudolf Steiner. However there existed the possibility to buy an evening's leave for the Pape soldiers for ten gold marks. So I went to the barracks and bought two evening leaves for Herr Hummel. In this way the money for The *Philosophy of Freedom* really obtained freedom.

The Death of Ernst Haeckel (9 August 1919)

Shortly after the death of Ernst Haeckel, probably at the beginning of September, we were sitting at the table in the Motzstrasse with Doctor and Frau Steiner just after we had had lunch. Also present was Frau Clara Walther. While we were drinking coffee I fetched the Berlin newspaper where the death of the great scientist was announced in big letters. Rudolf Steiner read this announcement to us and afterwards spoke in a very moving way about the life and work of Haeckel. He also raised the question as to who would inherit Haeckel's works and his estate.

Suddenly he turned to Frau Steiner and again referred to his example, which was always that of the Goethe Archives in Weimar where the Goethe Society had no right to take decisions. Furthermore, he said to her, in front of us all, that they had this matter regarding their own affairs well in hand.[5]

Frau Steiner answered that she would ask the spiritual world that she might go before him. Marie Steiner's hand was lying on the table and the Doctor took it and said: 'No, my dear, you have to live twenty years longer in order to save my work.' Frau Steiner replied: 'That is terrible.' Doctor Steiner put his hand once more on hers and repeated: 'Yes, my dear, you must live twenty years longer in order to preserve my work. That is your karma.' Frau Steiner was quite devastated.[6]

The Bust

In the visitor's room in the Potsdamerstrasse house stood a plaster bust of Rudolf Steiner which had been a gift to him. I did not like it, because we had the Doctor with us, alive and quite different. Now, the Philosophic-Anthroposophic Publishing Company was to be moved to Dornach and we were all packing. I was packing all the documents and records when Dr Steiner came to me with the bust in his arm and said: 'Sam, I will give him to you as a souvenir.' I could just manage to say: 'Thanks, Herr Doctor.'

When Dr Steiner had left I took the bust into the big hall where, underneath the stage, there was a low room about 33 ft long. I opened the sliding door and crept in with the bust which I pushed right into the furthest corner — out of sight, out of mind.!

Six months later there were big gatherings in Berlin, and the Doctor came to them from Dornach. He went through all the rooms in the house as though looking for something, but finally asked me: 'Sam, where did you put the plaster bust?' I replied: 'Herr Doctor, I do not like it,' and admitted where it had got to. The Doctor stepped through the open hall door and called loudly into the house for Frau Steiner who had no idea why she was suddenly summoned so urgently. I could see a smile playing around his lips as he asked me to show Frau Steiner where I had put the bust. I gave Frau Steiner a sign to come to the stage, pushed the door aside and pointed: 'There, in the corner.' Frau Steiner bent down, looked underneath the stage, and was amazed. The Doctor laughed heartily and beamed — 'Dear Sam, I only wanted to know *what* you had done with it.' He likes to express his sense of humour in this way.

Life Partners

Rudolf Steiner had absolute trust in Marie Steiner. The first known will, made when she still had the name Marie von Sivers, began with the words: 'After my death Frl. Marie von Sivers shall have the authority to decree in my name. What she decides, shall be done in my name.' And it ends with the words: 'Marie von Sivers herself will always be with me, our union remains indissoluble.' (See Appendix) At one time (after the death of Rudolf Steiner) Marie Steiner showed me a letter by him, in which he pointed out how it had been decreed in the spiritual world that he could only fulfil his earthly task together with her.

This letter belonged to those very personal ones by Rudolf Steiner which Marie Steiner destroyed. When I asked her why she had done this as it was important that the members knew about it, she answered very decisively: 'I cannot expose such an intimate matter to this Society!'

The Doctor had very often to suffer from the shortcomings of people, as well as social difficulties. Once it broke out of him like a cry: 'I am also human.' He worried about Marie Steiner and the time he would not be around. He appealed to my loyalty to her and once expressed to me the fear that '...when I am no longer here they will take everything away from her, so that she won't know how to make ends meet.'

Such things were, even then, already foreshadowed.

Petition and Judgement of the Solothurn Court

On the second visit to Anna Samweber she chanced to speak about the attempts to interpret Rudolf Steiner's will after his death so that the bequest would go to the Anthroposophical Society rather than to Marie Steiner. The view was that the Society was the rightful heir to Dr Steiner's works and, later, this view was supported by the Vorstand on the basis of a statement made by Dr Steiner at the refounding of the Anthroposophical Society at Christmas 1923, which amounted in their opinion to an annulment of the actual will.

At that time Rudolf Steiner had introduced the publishing house of Marie Steiner as a sub-section of the Anthroposophical Society itself. Then at the General Meeting of the Anthroposophical Society on 29 June 1924 Rudolf Steiner's actual words were: 'Als zweites innerhalb der Bewegung haben wir den Philosophisch- Anthroposophischen Verlag, der ja jetzt nach Dornach übergesiedelt ist, und der nicht anders behandelt werden kann, als ein integrierter Teil anthroposophischen Bewegung selber...' *'Secondly, we have within the movement the Philosophic-Anthroposophic Publishing Company, which has now moved to Dornach, and which must be regarded as an integral part of the Anthroposophical movement itself...' Anna Samweber then produced a document of fourteen typescript pages which she herself had composed. On her own initiative she had written a petition and handed it to the high court of Solothurn on 8 January 1952, where legal proceedings were in progress as to the interpretation and probate of Rudolf Steiner's will. She asked me to read this document aloud, which I did, and afterwards she gave it to me to take to Switzerland. A few passages from this document which refer to the memories of Rudolf Steiner may now be recalled. Anna Samweber expressed great satisfaction that the then 'Swiss Court of Justice' had, through its verdict, completely upheld the will of Rudolf Steiner and*

Marie Steiner and its execution, against the mistaken objection of the then Vorstand of the Anthroposophical Society.

The style of the petition is like the personality of Anna Samweber herself — objective, decisive and, if necessary, prepared to fight. The following is from the original text:

It is not the purpose of my letter to prove, even partly, the mistakes and absurdities — not to use stronger words — contained in the reasoning of the Vorstand. All the documents are in the hands of the law-court. But I want to show from my personal experiences and knowledge of Rudolf Steiner that he was in no way unworldly and would not have forgotten to revoke the original will. Neither did he think of himself as being too deeply spiritual to disregard outer laws or social rules. In fact, the opposite was the case. In order to give examples from real life situations, which might clarify the way a person thinks, I have recorded the following experiences and I assure you that, without question, these accounts are absolutely true.

1. One day, after a lecture, Rudolf Steiner remained in his room. He held a document in his hand and was in discussion with the solicitor, Dr. Büttner, (a member of the Society) and thought that he still needed a notary's certificate. Dr Büttner offered to settle the matter for him but Dr Steiner replied: 'Thank you, Herr Dr Büttner, but that won't do. The matter could have legal consequences. If it came to court the judge could say that you were biased and, besides, it would be indiscreet of me because you are a member.' In fact, Dr Steiner went the next day to a solicitor outside the Society, in the Potsdamerstrasse.

2. When the working group of Dr Steiner moved into new accommodation in the Potsdamerstrasse in Berlin, the completed rent agreement was put before Dr Steiner. He read the document carefully (as he always did in such cases), took a pencil from his pocket, made a correction and put in 'with accommodation for the caretaker.' This attention and exactness of Dr Steiner later had the effect, in a time of severe housing shortage when business rooms were confiscated and made into living

quarters, that the working group could keep their rooms.

3. .... (not recorded).

4. When Dr Steiner moved to Dornach and dissolved his household in Berlin, he made his study in the small hall which had been furnished and paid for by Frau Steiner. But the head of the group, who had already been chosen, did not take kindly to the fact that the furniture had ben moved without his knowledge. I was disgusted, and declared, in front of the gathered group, that if he did not like the Doctor's furniture standing in one of Dr Steiner's own rooms, then he could take his possessions: lamps, bucket and floorcloth (which he had bought) and go, as everything else belonged to Dr Steiner or Frau Steiner. When I told Dr Steiner in Stuttgart about this incident he spoke the words to Frau Steiner in a hurt tone: 'You see, my dear, these gentlemen are of the opinion that we are obliged to beg them to allow us to put our possessions into our own rooms.'

5. With the same strict exactness with which Dr Steiner treated the outer, mundane side of life in respect of ownership, he reacted to the smallest details of daily life.

During the almost eight years in which I lived in the house of Dr Steiner, I was often witness to the Philosophic-Anthroposophic publishers receiving boxes of newly-printed cycles and books of Rudolf Steiner from the printers. In spite of the fact that Rudolf Steiner — who was entitled to his royalties — and Frau Steiner — who owned the publishing company and had to pay them — were married and could be expected to have a more familiar way of dealing with the money side, there was a very clear division in financial matters. Every time, after the arrival of the books, Frl. Mücke, the treasurer of the company, went to Dr Steiner and paid him the renumeration due. Thanks to the particular manner of Frl. Mücke, the procedure went like this: Dr Steiner received the money, counted it, signed for it and thanked Frl. Mücke. Frl. Mücke dismissively said: 'It is you we have to thank', to which Dr Steiner replied: 'No, I thank you.'

6. Over ten years I had to make several typescript copies

of lectures by Dr Steiner from shorthand notes. On one of these occasions a member of the committee of the Munich branch came to me with the request to make a copy for her with the others. I asked Frau Steiner whether I was allowed to do that and she said I had to ask Dr Steiner as she could not make the decision. When I went to Dr Steiner to repeat my question he became almost angry that a possibility might exist that copies of his lecture could be passed on without his knowledge. He said: 'That is spiritual theft.' I made my excuse saying that that was why I had asked. He replied that he had had to speak so sharply as I should have known it myself.

7. When the Kommende Tag publishing house had been founded, Rudolf Steiner gave some of his books to these publishers to be printed, in order to give them a start. This, however, had the effect of their gradually absorbing the Philosophic-Anthoposophic Publishing Company of Frau Steiner and degrading it to mere distribution. (I do not think I need to point out to the court that the Philosophic-Anthroposophic Press had been funded with the money from Frau Steiner and had always managed quite well without any outside help.) In consequence of this newly-created false situation, Wolfgang Wachsmuth, the head of the Kommende Tag Press was called to Berlin by Dr Steiner (shortly before the 1923 Christmas Conference). Wolfgang Wachsmuth came down from the upper floor where the interview had taken place and asked me to take some papers regarding the matter to Dr Steiner on the second floor. When I entered the room Rudolf Steiner, walking to and fro in great indignation, threw the papers on the table and said: 'This band of robbers! They will not get another book from me! This Press is in dirty competition against the Philosophic-Anthoposophic Press of Frau Steiner! I won't let them take the clothes off her back. This is spiritual theft. We give this company everything, but they want to swallow us, lock, stock and barrel, and I will not allow it!'

These words stand out clearly in my memory because never before and never afterwards did I see Rudolf Steiner in such an indignant mood. I am describing this scene now, openly, because it shows clearly where Dr Steiner stood in the matter of ownership, and it also shows that it could never have occurred to him to leave his spiritual possessions to the Society as such or, because of the Christmas Conference or for any other reason, to have disregarded his precise will and made the Society his heir without this being clearly indicated.

With this report from the life with Dr Steiner I have attempted to show how absolutely correct and clear he was in his dealings with the outer things of daily life. He always read very carefully before he signed anything and never relied on others. He respected exactly the boundary between his possessions and the possessions of others; for example, he did not allow any unclarity in regard to legal and property matters, either because of a personal attachment to a person or because of a personal connection within a society. He protected his copyrights objectively and energetically, as he was strongly opposed to any vague attitude in these matters.

Scarf, Hat and Coat

When Rudolf Steiner gave one of his big public lectures at a time when he spoke up for the Threefold Social Order, he always used a special exit which led to the artists' room, from where I accompanied him through a long passage to the main exit. After one of these lectures there were many people standing around who wanted to put their questions and problems to him, and who occupied him for a long time. I was waiting by the side entrance and I had already got his coat, scarf and hat and was holding them in my arm so that I could pass them to him when he was finally free. After I had stood by the door for some time, he came, took his things from me, went back to the artists' room and put everything back on the hooks.

Then he took one piece after the other and put them on. With great surprise I burst out: 'But Herr Doctor, can you imagine how I feel?' He replied: 'And can you imagine how I feel?' We went silently through the dark corridor where I usually led him, as his eyesight was very bad in the dark, when suddenly he said 'Are you so angry with me that you let me walk into the wall?' Further on, he asked whether I did not know why he had acted like that. When I answered in the negative he replied: 'Think about it.'

When he met me the next day and the day after that his first question was: 'Have you thought about it?' I became quite upset and when I woke again at night, it came to me. When the people stood around Dr Steiner and besieged him, I had stood self-satisfied with the thought that I had *his* coat, *his* hat, *his* scarf. On the following day Dr Steiner asked me for the fourth time whether I had thought about it. I said: 'Yes, Herr Doctor, I know now why.' He answered: 'You see, Sam, that must not be.' He disliked intensely all personal cult and he gave it no chance to develop around him.

The Mysterious Visitor

One day an elegant gentleman appeared in the Potsdamerstrasse headquarters of the Berlin branch. He seemed to me of a southern type and wanted to speak to Rudolf Steiner. I said that he was not here. He was, however, not discouraged and pressed the point that what he had to discuss with Rudolf Steiner was very important. I declared myself willing to drive with him to the Motzstrasse, where the Doctor stayed. I noticed in the taxi on the way how this foreigner was murmuring mantrams all the time. I thought that weird and did not altogether trust him. When we arrived in the Motzstrasse I did not take him to Dr Steiner on the second floor but to the office of Herr

Walther on the first floor. I asked Herr Walther to announce the stranger with his card to Dr Steiner. Herr Walther returned with a definite refusal that Rudolf Steiner could not see the man. He had to leave without having achieved anything. Some time later the Doctor came down to us and said very intently: 'Sam, you have saved my life...', and thanked me. He indicated that an attack against him had been averted.

The Kitchen Table

In the kitchen stands a table which I call my 'holy table'. Come and look at it. (*Anna Samweber led the way and in her cheerful, positive way pointed to the old massive table made from dark hardwood*). From my story you will understand why it is the 'holy table' for me.

The Doctor was lecturing about the Michael Mystery and mission in the Berlin branch at the Potsdamerstrasse, where I had a small flat at the time. I was deeply touched and moved by the lecture, and afterwards Rudolf Steiner had to answer many questions by members. It was well after midnight by the time everybody had left. Then he came to me and sat at this table saying: 'Sam, you wanted to ask me something, too.' I had always tried not to burden the Doctor with my personal questions, so I said: 'No, Herr Doctor.' But he replied: 'Yes, Sam, please ask me your question!' 'Well, then, Herr Doctor,' I answered hesitatingly, 'during your lecture the question came to me: Who are you? Who were you? Who will you be?' The Doctor responded immediately and drew in front of me a curve on the table:

That is how his individuality ran like a red thread through the whole earth development and had been there before its beginning. He went on with these words: 'If you ponder on this with love and enthusiasm, you will find, even in this life, who I am.' I asked further: 'Shall we meet again?' And he replied: 'If you ponder on who I am with love and enthusiasm, we shall meet again.' The conversation at this table continued and I remember that he said on this occasion: 'When Christ walked on the earth and a person walked past Him, looked into His eyes and recognized Him, he became a Christian in his next life.' So, now you know why this is my 'holy table'.

Miscellaneous

When, after a lecture in the Potdamerstrasse, I accompanied Rudolf Steiner on his way home to the Motzstrasse, we passed near the Polish Embassy. Suddenly the Doctor stopped and said very seriously: 'It will not be long before there will not be one stone left upon another.' At that time I could not understand what he meant, but I remembered his words later, when I lived in destroyed Berlin, particularly when I walked through a completely demolished part of what had been the Polish Embassy.

Once Rudolf Steiner mentioned that the year 1984 would be a particularly difficult one.

Occasionally he expressed his thoughts to us, which fell like seeds. So he said once, while we stood at the stop waiting for a tramcar:

Without threefold social order — Bolshevism
Without Anthroposophy — Catholicism.

Of his book *Knowledge of the Higher Worlds*, he once said that it was suitable only for personal study; everything else one could work on in groups.

On the inside of his cupboard door the Doctor had written birthday dates. He valued the celebration of people's birthdays and remarked: 'In the night which follows a birthday that person is nearest to his "protecting spiritual being" and can converse with him (in his sleep) as from one person to another.'

At the Turn of the Year 1922

Before Christmas 1922 I was quietly harbouring the wish to be able to travel to Dornach in order to take part in the Christmas Conference. But it was the time of inflation and my finances had melted away. Also I owed the money for a large dentist's bill, the result of an accident. At the beginning of December Dr and Frau Steiner were staying in Berlin. Frau Steiner, who was always concerned with our well-being, personally paid the dentists's bill for me and said that this time I had to forgo the journey to Dornach because she had already promised Fräulein Tolch, the other co-worker in the Motzstrasse, to cover the cost of the journey to Dornach; there was not enough now for both of us. I was very sad and also uneasy because I had a clear premonition that the first Goetheanum would be destroyed. (This came from an inborn second sight which appeared in me at different times in my life.) Soon after the refusal by Frau Steiner I met Rudolf Steiner on the stairs. I told him about my sorrow and asked him for his advice. He tried to console me by pointing to the Easter Conference when I could see his fifth Mystery Drama. Also Frau Steiner had a lot of expense at present and had decided it that way. Then I burst out: 'Herr Doctor, you did say that if one walked once through the West-East axis of the "Bau" in a perceptive way that it would be an essential factor for the person after his death. And if I cannot go at Christmas I will never see the "Bau" again. We will lose it. It will be burnt, and at Easter it will not be there any more.' The Doctor looked at me in surprise but did not remark on my revelation in any way. He again pointed to the Easter Conference and said he was unable to help me now. I had to see whether any other possibility might arise.

Dr and Frau Steiner then left and I remained with my problem. Because I was the branch secretary I was often in touch with the Swiss Embassy in Berlin in order to get visas, which had to be paid for even then. One day I went to the Embassy and spoke to the official I knew. He was prepared to get me a free visa for entering Switzerland. I mentioned that I had first to find a way to get the money for the ticket as I was very determined to go on this journey.

The following day I had a call from this official: 'Fräulein Samweber, you are lucky! We still need somebody to accompany sick children for the Red Cross from Berlin to Basel after Christmas. Will you take this on?' What a lucky chance! Of course, I agreed immediately. Towards the end of December we journeyed to Basel where I delivered the children and then made my way to Dornach. When I went to greet Rudolf Steiner after the lecture, he welcomed me with joy and warmth and enquired about my accommodation. When I told him that I had none as yet, he saw to it that I could stay in the house of the van der Pals family.

In the afternoon of New Year's Eve I walked with Herr Gern and Herr Drescher towards the Gempenberg. I was extremely restless, and when we saw the landscape with the Goetheanum below us I spoke to my companions of my strong premonitions about the 'Bau'. But Herr Gern's reaction seemed to be that this was abnormal.

In the evening I heard the lecture by Rudolf Steiner in the Goetheanum *The Spiritual Communion of Mankind*. Afterwards I declined an invitation to a New Year's Eve gathering with Herr and Frau Walther, my Berlin friends, and Frau Fink, and instead went to my room in the house of van der Pals. Some time later I heard Herr van der Pals give the alarm: 'The "Bau" is burning, let's go up quickly!' So it happened that I spend the night of the New Year at the burning Goetheanum helping to save what was possible. There was the danger that the 'Schreinerei', with the halls and Rudolf Steiner's studio, which stood above the Goetheanum, might catch fire. In it was the large wooden statue on which Dr Steiner had worked for a long time and which was to be placed in a central position in the Goetheanum after its completion. It was nine metres high, and could be dismantled. Young people carried the pieces into the open and put them on the lawn against the de Jaager's house. Rudolf Steiner put me to stand guard on these wooden pieces and so I saw, as it were past the raised arm of the Christ statue, the consuming flames raging. For a while I became aware of Rudolf Steiner standing not far from me with Miss Maryon and Frau de Jaager in front of their house entrance. When the dome crashed down with a loud noise and huge flames shot up, I was overwhelmed by a spiritual experience. I saw the 'Bau' high above the burning place, shining brilliantly white, and I felt with certainty that something stupendous was happening here. From below, the colours of the metal organ pipes glowed in the flames and I heard a sound but, at the same time, a shrill cry. When I looked to the other side, to the de Jaagers house, I saw Rudolf Steiner surrounded by a huge white aura of light. I called to my co-watchers: 'Look at the Doctor!', and I knew something was happening between the Doctor and the burning building. My companions did not notice this and the picture vanished.

In the morning I saw Rudolf Steiner waving to me to go to him. He asked me to go to Frau Steiner in the Hansi's house and stay with her. At that time she had difficulty in walking, therefore she had experienced the fire in the night from below in the garden and was deeply shaken. When I arrived at the house, she greeted me with the words: 'I am so happy that you are here.' I stayed with her for the next few days and helped where help was needed. Frau Steiner treated me with great kindness and gave me many beautiful presents before my departure to Berlin.

A wonderful chain of coincidences had brought me here from Berlin so that I might still see the first Goetheanum, and I was also privileged to take part in those heavy hours of destiny of Rudolf and Marie Steiner.

In the Hall of the Berlin Philharmonic

It was the time when Rudolf Steiner was working publicly for the idea of the Threefold Social Order. Between the Communist and National Socialist extremes he put this social idea of the middle way and spoke about it in various parts of Berlin. I always helped enthusiastically, giving out handbills announcing meetings, and the interest of a number of workmen was aroused. Through the concert agency Wolff and Sachs, which organized not only concerts but also big lectures, the hall of the Philharmonic was hired for a Threefold Social Order lecture. The organizers and the management directors had received threatening letters calling for Steiner's appearance to be prevented.

When I went to the management of the Philharmonic on the day before the lecture, my attention was emphatically drawn to the danger surrounding the event. Without notifying Dr Steiner the C.I.D. was called to protect the hall and their officials were posted also by the main switchboard in the cellar. I enquired about the possibility of Rudolf Steiner not entering through the main entrance but using another entrance and exit. There was one that led from the artists' room through the yard to the harbour area, and in this way Dr Steiner would not be exposed to the great pressure from the public. The huge hall was sold out and it was arranged that members of the Berlin branch of the Society would take their seats on the stage behind the speaker's lectern in case he needed protecting. In addition I had asked a workman I knew, who was strong and athletic, to position himself on the stage and, if necessary, secure the way to the artists' room for Rudolf Steiner.

After all these preparations I went to the Motzstrasse to Dr and Frau Steiner and reported that the Philharmonic hall was sold out, but kept secret the preparations which had been made. I only asked Rudolf Steiner to use the back entrance so that Frau Steiner would not be exposed to the pressure from the public. He replied, however: 'Well, you and Frau Steiner can use the back entrance, I will drive up in front.' When I did not give in, he said: 'Why do you want to deceive me? You see, for this evening I am the employee of the firm Wolff and Sachs. They provide the car. Ask the firm.' But it had all been arranged with the firm, so Rudolf Steiner agreed to use the back entrance.

The hall was more than full and the last tickets were sold at black market prices. In such lectures at big events Rudolf Steiner often spoke very directly and made no concessions to popular, sensational expectations. So also on this evening. He spoke with resonance and resolution.

At the end of the lecture I went immediately with Rudolf Steiner to the artists' room. He shut the door behind us, turned the key and said: 'Don't call anybody.' Then he dropped to the floor like one dead. I got a deep shock and thought: This is the end. His countenance seemed very old, as touched by death. He lay like that for some minutes, which seemed to me much longer. Suddenly he began to move, got up on his own and then said to me: 'I have fought with demons but I have conquered them.' When somebody knocked on the door he asked who was there, and when Emil Leinhas announced himself he went to open the door personally.

For the Berlin Friends

At the end of October 1923 I was on holiday in Dornach and took part in the watch on the area of the Goetheanum. The burning of the Goetheanum and other indications demanded a protective watch on the Schreinerei area and also Rudolf Steiner's studio. At a late hour on a cold November night I walked around the ruins of the Goetheanum (the concrete foundations were still standing). I noticed on my round that the light was still on in Rudolf Steiner's studio although it was after midnight. On a later round, towards four in the morning, it had been extinguished and Rudolf Steiner had gone down to the Hansi's house. Suddenly, I stood still on my path like one spellbound. I had a flaming vision: Berlin stood in bright flames! Under the impression of this strong experience I asked Rudolf Steiner the next day for an interview. He gave me an appointment for the following morning at eleven o'clock in the studio. I told him about my experience in the night and added: 'Anthroposophy is like a cup from which we can always drink anew. Once the hard times come over us and we not longer have you with us any more, Herr Doctor, can you give us some helping words for that?' Rudolf Steiner answered in the affirmative and gave me a time when I could collect his answer from the studio.

The following day (probably 10 November) I stood in front of the black announcement board in the Schreinerei and read the notice about the 'March to the Feldherrnhalle' in Munich; the first public impact of the National Socialists. Rudolf Steiner then joined us, read the notice, and said to those of us who were standing around: 'If these gentlemen get into the government, I will no longer be able to set foot on German soil.' Then he turned to me and said, 'Sam, please come this afternoon at five o'clock for tea to the Hansi's house!' When I got there at the given time, Frau Steiner was sitting at the table taking coffee. She said to me: 'The Doctor has told me that you have asked him for something. He was very pleased about your request.' Soon Rudolf Steiner entered with several papers under his arm. From these he handed me a letter and said: 'Sam, I have to ask you to travel to Berlin this evening to see to some urgent business.' I was surprised and replied: 'Herr Doctor, I am still on holiday for a few days and would like to spend them here.' He opened a document — the lease on the Berlin apartments; he had written to Fräulein Mücke asking her to give notice to give the apartments up. 'Yes, Sam, you must do this for my sake.' Frau Steiner was rather upset, for they had built the hall there and now it had to be rebuilt into flats. Then the Doctor repeated the words which he had spoken by the blackboard: 'Yes, Frau Steiner, if these men come to power, neither of us could tread on German soil any more.' Doctor and Frau Steiner were very solemn when later we drove up to the Schreinerei to a performance. Doctor Steiner went into his studio, and I accompanied Frau Steiner to her room in the Schreinerei and then took leave of her. I went into the studio as planned where I found Rudolf Steiner very solemn as he stood in front of the Christ-statue. On the table lay the verses he had written for me. When he handed me the sheet, he declared: 'Yes, Sam, there is much suffering in these lines, but the hour will come when you all will read between the lines of worse sufferings.' He placed my hands on his breast and continued: 'Tell the Berlin friends...I will then be amongst you!' He made signs on my forehead and breast: 'Sam, I need faithful, courageous people. Remain courageous and faithful.' As a farewell he kissed me on the forehead and requested: 'I want Frau Steiner to say farewell to you!' I replied that I had done that before, but he repeated his request and came with me to the room of Frau Steiner and asked her to kiss me goodbye. Then I left the Schreinerei and took the night train to Berlin to fulfil the commission of Rudolf Steiner.[7]

The following is the verse[8] for the Berlin friends which Rudolf Steiner gave to Anna Samweber in 1923:

Den Berliner Freunden

Es siehet der Mensch
Mit dem welt' erzeugten Auge;
Ihn bindet, was er siehet,
An Weltefreude und Weltenschmerz,
Es bindet ihn an alles,
Was da wird, aber minder nicht
An alles, was da stürzet
In Abgrundes finstre Reiche.

Es schauet der Mensch
Mit dem geist'verlieh'nen Auge;
Ihn bindet, was er schauet,
An Geisteshoffen und Geistes-Halte-Kraft,
Es bindet ihn an alles,
Was in Ewigkeiten wurzelt
Und in Ewigkeiten Früchte trägt.

Aber schauen kann der Mensch
Nur, wenn er des Inneren Auge
Selber Fühlet als Geistes-Gottes-Glied,
Das auf der Seele Schauplatz
Im Menschen-Leibes-Tempel
Der Götter Taten wirket.

Es ist die Menschheit
Im Vergessen an das Gottes-Innre,
Wir aber wollen es nehmen
In des Bewusstseins helles Licht,
Und dann tragen über Schutt und Asche

Der Götter Flamme im Menschenherzen.
So Mögen Blitze unsre Sinneshäuser
In Schutt zerschmettern:
Wir errichten Seelehnäuser
Aus der Erkenntnis Eisenfestem Lichtesweben,
Und Untergang des Äussern
Soll werden Aufgang
Des Seelen-Innersten.

Das leid dringet heran
Aus Stoffes-Kraft-Gewalten;
Die Hoffnung leuchtet,
Auch wenn Finsternis uns umwallt;
Und sie wird dereinst
In Unsre Erinnerung dringen,
Wen wir nach der Finsternis
Im Lichte wieder leben dürfen.
Wir wollen nicht, dass diese Leuchte
Dereinst in Künft'gen Helligkeiten uns fehle,
Weil wir sie jetzt im Leide
Nicht in unsre Seelen eingepflanzet haben.

To the Berlin Friends

Man looks out
With the world-engendered eye,
And what he sees thus binds him
To world delight and world despair.
It binds him unto all
That springs to life there, but not less
To all that plunges there
Into the dark abyss.

But man beholds
With the spirit-entrusted eye.
What he beholds thus binds him

To spirit hope and spirit's upholding power.
It binds him unto all
That roots within eternity
And bears within eternity its fruits.

Yet man can only then behold
When he feels the inner eye
Itself as God-given spirit organ,
Which at the focus of the soul,
Within the temple of man's body,
Fulfils the deed of gods.

Mankind is in forgetfulness
Of the Godhead's innermost.
We, though, will raise it and take it
Into our consciousness, flood with light
And then bear it over dust and ashes —
The divine flame in the human heart.

So may the lightning shatter into dust
Our sense/built houses.
We will erect instead soul houses
Built on knowledge,
Upon its iron-firm, light-woven web.
And downfall of the outer
Shall become uprise
Of the soul's own innermost.

For pain passes upon us
From powers of material force,
But hope illumines
Even when darkness enshrouds us,
And it will one day
Emerge within our memory
When at length, after the darkness,
We may live again in light.

We do not want this clear illumining
To be in future brightnesses denied us
Because we have not now,
In pain, implanted it within our souls.

True Discipleship

Dr Carl Unger and his strict interpretations of Anthroposophy, although greatly valued by Rudolf Steiner, were rejected in some circles of the youth movement[9] and there was quite a campaign against him from the younger element. Carl Unger was a leading member of the German Council of the Anthroposophical Society, and in a General Assembly of the German Society, where I was also present, he spoke about these problems. At one point Rudolf Steiner interrupted him abruptly and announced, amidst general surprise, that he would set up a separate social organization in order to meet the opposition. (This was to be called 'Free Society'.) Dr Unger had by then gone back to his place and some of his opponents were triumphant. There followed a short interval and then the leaders of the youth movement spoke again, followed by Dr Steiner. After that there was a second interval when I went to see Frau Steiner in her room in the Gustav Siegle house. In order to get back into the hall I used the way via the stage, which I knew well. When I was about to go through I noticed Rudolf Steiner and Dr Unger standing in conversation by themselves. I hesitated to go on and inadvertently became witness to Rudolf Steiner saying to Dr Unger: 'You will want to take some time off for a holiday?' But Dr Unger replied: 'No, I will remain in my place!' Dr Steiner was clearly moved and, embracing him, kissed him on the forehead and said to him: 'You have passed the hardest test! You are my true disciple!'

After the Assembly I noticed how many people made a point of cutting Dr Unger. However, I went to him and asked whether I might drive home with him. He agreed, and within his family circle I saw how he rose over the evening's incident and the human frailties which he had witnessed.

Even from his sick-bed Rudolf Steiner requested Marie Steiner repeatedly (also by letter when she was on tour) to stand up for Dr Unger and repudiate the campaign against him. In a later obituary (24.2.1929) Marie Steiner wrote about Dr

Unger: '... vague, emotional mysticism should submit to the strict practice of forming objective, logical concepts...' The rejection of this way of thinking of Dr Unger's increased to a kind of rejection of him as a person. It was said that it was too dry, too matter of fact, too abstract. These judgements sounded strange to those who knew him better and had experienced the opposite. But this mood came to a climax in a kind of persecution. He was made out to be a danger to the development of our Society, which would not accommodate the direction taken by him for the spiritual work. The widespread whispering campaign made out that his spiritual approach was little short of being pernicious. But his was the approach that Rudolf Steiner expected from his co-workers, without which he did not think a healthy development of our movement possible.

On the Death of Carl Unger

On 13 December 1928 Dr Carl Unger gave a public lecture in Berlin, and on the following evening a lecture to the members about esotericism.[10] In this last lecture he also spoke in favour of the publication of certain esoteric texts in order to prevent their misuse. There followed turmoil in the hall, during which I had a terrible inner experience: Suddenly I heard three shots and saw Dr Unger collapse over the lectern. The vision passed quickly and I saw and heard Dr Unger speaking as before. But in me there was the certainly — Carl Unger will be killed.

After the lecture I went with about thirty friends and Dr Unger to a café. The conversation went on about matters and worries of the Anthroposophical Movement and the Society, leading on to the impending Easter Conference in Dornach. Dr Unger expressed the need to tackle existing conflicts courageously. He asked me to go to Dornach, whatever happened. When I replied that I did not know whether this was possible (financially) he said: 'That is my concern, but I need people with courage!'

When we left the restaurant Dr Unger and I went the same way at first towards the Potsdamer Platz. I told him that after his explanations I, too, thought it right to publish the aforementioned texts, and asked him whether he had spoken to Frau Steiner about the whole matter. He answered in the negative, saying that he had assumed the responsibility himself. Soon, however — in fact, at Christmas — he was going to Dornach and would do it then, because the publication had to proceed. In front of the Fürstenhof hotel, where Dr Unger was staying, I took courage and said: 'Herr Dr Unger, I would like to tell you something very important and personal, and in confidence, but I do not want to do it here in the street.' In his rooms I started again: 'Herr Dr Unger, I beg you to clear up and put in order the matter with the German Society and the texts in Dornach at Christmas.' He raised the objection that such a matter with the German Society could probably only be settled at Easter at the General Assembly. I replied: 'Herr Dr Unger, we have no time. Settle everything at Christmas. We shall lose you...You will be shot...'

He took my forewarning with all seriousness, looked at me very earnestly and answered: 'If that is true, I will then try at Christmas in Dornach to settle the matter with the German Society.'

We shook hands on leaving. He accompanied me down to the entrance. It was our last meeting.

In Dornach at Christmas Dr Unger really tried to settle things. He suggested to his opponents in the Council of the German Society, Dr. Kolisko and Dr Stein, that they resign. When he did not succeed, Dr Unger resigned, not only from the Council but also as a member of the German Society.

At Christmas and New Year's Eve I usually invited members of the Society in Berlin who had no family. We met in the Potsdamerstrasse where I had a little flat near the office and the members' rooms. So it happened that year, too, that I planned for our circle of friends to celebrate the entry into the New Year together.

When the bells rang in the New Year, I opened the window — an old family custom — and, with my hand pointing outside, called: 'Old Year go out!'; and with a welcoming gesture I called: 'New Year come in!'.

At this moment I again heard the three shots and once more had that terrible vision. Very upset, I called to the friends: 'We will lose Dr Unger.' Our party broke up soon after that and the friends left.

Some days later, on 4 January 1929, there was an internal conference, for which I had to heat the hall. When I entered the hall just after half-past seven I experienced for the third time Dr Unger's death. After the conference, late in the evening, I received a call from the Secretariat of the Anthroposophical Society. I was asked for information about a certain Dr Unger who had been shot[11] that evening in Nuremberg, where he was about to give a lecture on Anthroposophy. The next morning several newspapers also phoned.

Carl Unger had left me a letter, in which he said that at a meeting with Marie Steiner in Dornach they had come to a mutual understanding; also that he had settled the matter with the German Society.

Marie Steiner called Carl Unger 'the first martyr of the new spiritual movement.'

Later Experiences

It was in the twenties that I came across a newspaper article which announced that a Polish farm worker had appeared in Germany, who passed herself off as Anastasia, the daughter of the late Tsar. Because of my, earlier mentioned, meeting with the family of the Tsar in Odessa I felt obliged to follow this matter up.

During my investigations I came upon the aristocratic family of von Altenburg who were closely related to the Tsarina. Through a connection I was able to get an invitation to a reception, to which the so-called Anastasia was expected to be present. When I saw her and spoke with her I had hardly any doubt that it was her. However, I kept quiet about my stay in Odessa and my experience in the royal train. For some time 'Anastasia' lived in Berlin at the Danish Embassy. Before I could give definite proof of her identity I wanted to examine everything very carefully. Through the good offices of a Mr Vett I was able to visit her which gave me the opportunity, on Christmas Eve, to invite her to my flat. On that occasion Anastasia came to speak of her memories and mentioned Odessa. She then started to tell me about her family's visit in 1914 and the events in the royal train. She recalled the scene of the children's reception exactly and of how, because she took a chocolate, her mother had slapped her hand in front of everyone present. This was for me irrefutable evidence that she must be the real Anastasia. Now I could reveal myself as the teacher who had come into the carriage with a small delegation of children. Also, I still had the photograph taken at that time.

During that evening she told me about the executions in the cellar at Ekaterinburg where all her family were shot. She had stood in front of an older sister and probably was only grazed by a bullet, but had fallen with the others and lost consciousness. The men who took away the bodies for cremation must suddenly have noticed that one girl was only wounded and was still alive. Now one has to know the Russian; he shoots when he is commanded to do so, but to murder a wounded, whimpering child — there the heart speaks and pity acts.

The von Altenburg family helped Anastasia with all their means to file a lawsuit for the recognition of her name and her succession. The huge assets of the Tsar's family had been deposited with the Bank of England and the youngest brother of the Tsar, Grand Duke Cyrill, who lived with his wife in Paris at the time, had fought for a long time for his inheritance. Cyrill's wife was the most vehement opponent of Anastasia, while Cyrill himself seemed to be convinced of her identity. Since Anastasia spoke only the Russian of the ordinary people, this was seen as a reason to eliminate her. Her mother, the Tsarina, was German, but had been brought up in England. I had witnessed myself that English and German were spoken at court and Anastasia remembered these languages quite well. I was also called as a witness at the trial, where the photograph of the Tsar's family in 1914 and my evidence had a strong influence on the proceedings.

One day Anastasia and I passed a cinema in Berlin near the Zoo station where the current film 'Rasputin' was advertised with a huge portrait poster of Rasputin outside. When Anastasia saw it, she cried out: 'The Holy Man!' and collapsed unconscious beside me. In spite of efforts to revive her, she only gained consciousness after about two hours.

The trial went on for years. World War II came and interrupted it, and it was only some time after the end of the war that the lawsuit was taken up anew. By now Anastasia was oppressed by the publicity when she agreed to sell her experiences to a film company. With the proceeds and with the help of her friends she was able to lead a modest retiring existence in a house in Southern Germany near Unterlengenhardt. The trial went on. Some time ago, judges from England visited me for some hours and I gave them all the information I could. I learned then about a letter from the Grand Duke Cyrill to Jussupo in which he suggested an indemnity for Anastasia. When the proposal went to Anastasia she declined it with the words: 'I do not want money, I want my name!'[12]

Workings of Destiny

At the end of the second world war, when the Russians pushed into destroyed Berlin, I was staying in that part of the building in the Motzstrasse which was still habitable. I encouraged the women and mothers there by assuring them that I would stand up to the Russians and protect them. I stationed myself in the yard below and when they approached I cried out loud in Russian that they would not find any enemies here. I spoke to their consciences by telling them to leave these unprotected mothers alone. Their leader, a sturdy officer, came to me and asked whether I came from Odessa, and in conversation he declared that he had been a pupil in a German school for a time and knew me from then. Full of joy he picked me up and held me up in front of his soldiers and called: 'Look, this is my teacher!' In this way we were all saved and even got food from them. In consequence I was used as an interpreter for the Russians, and in this capacity was able to gain a measure of relief for some of the people of Berlin.

Because of my activities and connections I got this lovely flat here in the Lessing-Nicolai house which is protected by an ancient monument trust. At the time when Lessing was in Berlin he lived here and in this lovely room where we are at present he translated Shakespeare. (Friedrich Nicolai with Lessing and Moses Mendelsohn, his close friends, had founded the Library of the 'Schöne Wissenschaften and freie Künste'.)

It was two years ago when, one day, I met a young foreigner by the entrance downstairs with a travel book in his hand, who was looking for something. He addressed me with the words: 'Is this the Lessing Nicolai house?' I answered in the affirmative and saw that he was Russian. We started to speak in Russian and we soon found ourselves in a lively conversation. He turned out to be an officer in the Engineers and had a few days leave. It transpired that he had been born in Odessa, and when I asked him the name of the street it was the same which I had lived in when I was there. On asking further after the house, it turned out that he had been born and grew up in the same one where I had lived with the shipowner's family. He was a religious and pious person and we talked with mutual understanding about Christ and Christianity. On leaving he blessed me with the sign of the cross. Some months later he sent me the promised picture cards of Odessa and also a photograph of our 'common' house.

It is now several years since I received a request to vacate 'as soon as possible' the flat in the Lessing house, as it had to be renovated. Here I had settled so well with some of the furniture inherited from Rudolf Steiner; also his Sistine *Madonna* which hung on the wall. The day came when the state building official arrived in order to look at the flat and the house and to fix the date of the move. There was also a picture of Rudolf Steiner in my apartment and, when this official inspected the rooms, he stopped in front of it, looked at it for a while and said to me: 'My parents had this picture of Rudolf Steiner hanging in their house — they revered him — Frau Samweber, I will do everything I can so that you can move into another apartment in this big house while yours is being renovated' — and he actually managed it.

My stay in this house came into question a second time, as it was now intended to turn it into a museum. So another official came to move me out. While I was talking to him his eyes alighted on a special pendant which was on a necklace around my neck. Suddenly he asked where I had got that pendant from. I told him that it was a present from a Jewish lady whom I had been able to help before she was taken away to the concentration camp in Theresienstadt. He now revealed to me, full of emotion, that the lady who had owned this pendant, which he well remembered from his childhood, had been his mother and that she had perished in Theresienstadt. After further negotiations it transpired that he would do his very best to make it possible for me to stay in this flat; and so I am still here to this day, along with the chair from Rudolf Steiner's study.

Yes, in such a concrete way can one experience the workings of destiny!

Appendix

Further points from the will of Rudolf Steiner.

17 Motzstrasse, Berlin.
4 July 1910.
Will

With this I declare, as the signatory, that after my death the following are to be regarded as part of my last will and testament.

1. After my death all correspondence in my possession as well as all other written papers, documents and letters shall go to Fräulein Marie von Sivers, of 17 Motzstrasse, Berlin. She alone will determine, in the knowledge of my wishes, what shall be done with the said writings as well as with all documents now in my possession.

2. Fräulein Marie von Sivers shall be the sole administrator of all my literary estate after my death; she shall make decisions about new editions of my works as well as the publication of my manuscripts and lectures.

Dr Rudolf Steiner

After the marriage of Rudolf Steiner and Marie von Sivers another mutual will was drawn up in the presence of a Notary on 18 March 1915. It contains the same as the last with the addition in Article 4 which reads:

The partner who is left when the other one dies shall be the sole heir and is free to decide about the whole estate...

Translation of handwritten Will (Facsimile on page 49)

After my death Fräulein Marie von Sivers shall be my sole heir and have the right to decree in my name. Whatever she decides will in effect have been done in my name. All my possessions shall go to her and everything shall be done to her order. In particular, she should remember my parents and brother and sister in Horn. She shall regard my death as being in accordance with the wishes of higher powers and not look on it as a riddle. Such things occur in a context which must be respected, even if one cannot yet understand it.

Marie von Sivers herself will be with me always. Our union remains indissoluble.

Dr Rudolf Steiner

Berlin, 19 February 1907.

Nach meinem Tode soll Fräulein Marie von Sivers das Recht haben, in meinem Namen zu verfügen. Was sie so thut, soll in meinem Namen gethan sein. Das wenige, was ich besitze, geht alles in ihre Hände über; sie soll alle Verfügungen treffen. Insbesondere soll sie an meine Eltern und Geschwister in Horn denken.

Sie selbst soll meinen Tod als im Sinne höherer Mächte ansehen und ihn ja nicht als ein Räthsel ansehen. Die Dinge haben einen Zusammenhang, den man ehren muss, auch wenn man ihn noch nicht versteht.

Marie von Sivers selbst wird aber immer bei mir sein. Unsere Einigung bleibt unlöslich.

Dr. Rudolf Steiner

Berlin, 19. Februar 1907.

Notes

1. Anna Samwebers death occurred on 2 August 1969.
2. This was for Sophie Stinde. See *Gedenkworte Rudolf Steiners*, GA 261, Rudolf Steiner und unsere Toten, 30.11.1915.
3. From the 'World-Midnight' scene in Rudolf Steiner's Mystery Drama *The Soul's Awakening*.
4. Anna Samweber always wore the medal under her dress.
5. There existed a mutual will, agreed before a Notary Public on 18 March 1915, which gave the survivor the total inheritance and absolute right of decision on the disposal of the other's estate. (See also Appendix)
6. This report was given to the publisher by Frau Clara Walther — who was also present at the time — exactly in the same way, word for word. Marie Steiner also spoke of it to Emil Leinhas, her adviser in business matters. He repeats it in a shortened version in his book *Aus meiner Arbeit mit Rudolf Steiner* (Zbinden Verlag, Basel, 1950, p.32): 'Marie Steiner once expressed at the table that, for whatever reason, she did not want to survive Rudolf Steiner. She just could not imagine it. Rudolf Steiner said: "But yes, you will have to save my name!" When I reminded Marie Steiner of it in the year 1948, she replied: "Yes, he spoke of this to me repeatedly, even as early as Berlin."
7. Since Rudolf Steiner did not give any more lectures in Berlin, this was presumably Anna Samweber's last meeting with him.
8. English translation by Arvia MacKaye Ege, in *Truth-Wrought-Words*. Anthroposophic Press, New York, 1979.
9. Amongst the worries which came to Rudolf Steiner during his last years of activity (1923/24) were the difficulties between the older and younger generations, which were often connected with personalities. Rudolf Steiner highlighted this in the following words in Stuttgart (8

February 1923): 'Apart from the rights and wrongs it is, in a certain sense, the fact that such lack of understanding is mutual! These differences are not necessarily the fault of the older generation but more their destiny. The recalcitrance of youth is, at the same time, a defence and weakness.' And again, one year later, (News-sheet, 16 April 1924): 'Anthroposophy shall have no age; it lives in the eternal, which unites all people... Youth will wrestle in vain for true humanity if they try and flee that humanity of which they must eventually be a part.'

10. After the death of Rudolf Steiner it was a concern of Dr Carl Unger to keep alive in the Anthroposophical Society an understanding for the difference between the old and the new esotericism, as maintained by Rudolf Steiner, in order to exclude sectarianism. For that Dr Unger strove, especially in lectures of October and November 1928, when certain extremist elements came to the fore. There were different grades of development in esotericism but secrecy had no place: 'The esotericism of the present must be free, for only so can it be Christian; the old, restricted esotericism is luciferic. Behind the striving after secrecy in this area stands not a new but an old impulse — to gain superiority over others. And that works like poison in the social life of humanity.' (C Unger, *Schriften*, Vol. II, p.238.)
11. Dr Unger had been killed by the shots of a mentally sick person.
12. In the meantime Anastasia had married late in life and had gone to live in America, leaving her tragic destiny in Europe behind her. Anna Samweber knew her address and harboured a deep compassion for 'possibly the hardest destiny for a woman to bear in our century'.